Daddy lost his job

BARRON'S

Money, money, money!!! I never really thought about it until last week when Dad lost his job. That's when everything changed, including me! Instead of thinking about all the things that I wanted, like those black-and-white soccer shoes or that new video game, I started to think about the things we needed.

2-3

I'll never forget that day — it was the biggest snowstorm of the season! There was snow everywhere. There was so much snow that you couldn't even see across the street. The whole town had shut down. Everything was closed, even the restaurants. We were snowed in!!! And that meant it was a perfect day to snuggle up by the fire and watch movies.

And that's what we did! Dad and I built a fire, and Mom and my brother Ricky made the popcorn. Then we watched movies, played cards, and waited and waited for the snow to stop falling. It was the best day ever until...

...the phone rang. "I'll get it," said Dad as he rolled off the couch. A few minutes later, Dad came back. He had a funny look on his face, like he was scared.

"What happened?," Mom asked.

"I have some bad news," Dad said as he sat down on the couch beside me. "My company is trying to save money, so that means that a lot of people are losing their jobs and I'm one of them. I've lost my job!," Dad said.

At that moment, everything seemed to stop. It was as if time stood still. I couldn't hear the movie, the fire stopped crackling, and the popcorn that I had just eaten seemed to be stuck in the back of my throat. We sat in silence, each of us lost in our own thoughts, wondering: "What are we going to do?"

Then Mom stood up. "A snowy day isn't complete until we've had hot chocolate," Mom said as she headed to the kitchen.

"Cheer up guys," Dad said. "We'll figure things out, don't worry."

After a few days of being snowed in, the town was finally coming back to life and things were getting back to normal, except Dad did not have a job. I have to say that it was nice eating breakfast with Dad in the morning before we went to school. And, after school, when we came home, he was always waiting for us at the bus stop so that he could walk us home.

But when a few days turned into a few weeks and then a few months and Dad still did not have a job, I started to worry. I worried that we would not be able to stay in our house anymore or that we would not have enough money for food. And then I overheard Mom asking Dad, "What are we going to do?" That's when I really started to worry.

So, while Dad was busy looking for a job and Mom was busy looking after some of the neighborhood kids for extra money, Ricky and I came up with a plan, a plan to save money.

"It's called Operation Save," I said one night while we were sitting at the dinner table.

"Ricky and I have thought of some ways that we can save money," I said.

"And the secret to saving money is to spend less," said Ricky with a smile on his face.

18-19

From that day onward, Operation Save was in full swing.
That meant that whenever we wanted things, like a new pair of soccer
shoes, a new video game, or even going out for dinner, we would think
about it first. Was it something we really needed?

And guess what? We found out that, for a lot of the things we thought we needed, we really didn't need them at all. Ricky and I learned how to make the things we already had feel like new again. I shined up my soccer shoes and Ricky found an old video game from the back of the closet that we had forgotten about. We even started making our own lunches instead of buying lunch at school.

Even dinner turned into an adventure! Mom and Dad became good at using up leftovers. And to make dinner even better, Mom started to make up fancy names for everything she made. Who could have guessed that there were so many recipes for leftover chicken?

It seemed like Operation Save was really helping us. We didn't spend so much money on the things we didn't need, and we were still able to play soccer and go to the movies once in awhile. It wasn't so bad!

Then, one morning when Ricky and I came downstairs for breakfast, we found Dad in the kitchen making pancakes. He was wearing a fancy suit and tie with an apron wrapped around his waist.

"Are you feeling OK, Dad?," Ricky asked.

"I feel terrific!," Dad said as he flipped a pancake high up into the air. "Let's eat!," said Dad. "I have some good news!"

"Come on Dad, tell us the good news," I said as I finished off my last pancake.

"Ok, here it goes. I've got a job and I start today!," Dad smiled.

Ricky and I jumped up and shouted "Hooray!"

"I'm going to miss you, Dad," I said.

"Me too," Dad sighed. "But everything's going to be OK."

As I think back to that snowy day, a lot has changed. Dad has a job, Mom still looks after the neighborhood kids, and Operation Save has become a way of life for us. Maybe things really do happen for a reason!

Parents Guide

One of our responsibilities as parents is to provide for our children by making sure that their needs are met. In order to do so, however, we need money, financial stability, and jobs! Unfortunately, due to economic hardships, people are losing their jobs through no fault of their own, and some of these people are parents.

When a parent's job is suddenly ended with little or no warning, many things within the family are instantly hurt. For example, the family's lifestyle changes due to financial problems, which harms a sense of security.

In fact, everything changes — our focus shifts from all the things we thought we wanted to all the things we know we need. Even the roles within the family change. All of a sudden, the parent who used to get up every morning to go to work is at home looking after the household, filled with worry about looking for another job.

Speaking from personal experience, I know how difficult this situation can be and how the fear of the unknown can have a large impact on each member of the family, including the children.

Financial well being is threatened.

One way to reduce some of this anxiety is by including children in the "worrying" process by acknowledging the loss and then providing them with a chance to take part in the planning process of moving forward, in an age appropriate way.

Perhaps children can come up with different ways to save money, or to reduce some of the daily waste. Whatever they can do to help to make the situation better will give them a sense of control and worth.

When children are part of the plan, their readiness to give up some of their WANTS grows, and will not be considered a great sacrifice. They will feel good about themselves, and they might even recognize that perhaps they didn't really want what they thought they wanted after all.

Last but not least, remember that things will get better and you will find another job. It may take time, but try to be patient and keep your chin up. Life has a way of challenging us and keeping us on our toes; but, in the end, we become tougher, more creative, and despite everything...

Things will get better!

We learn a valuable life lesson: NEVER GIVE UP!

Daddy **lost** his job

Daddy lost his job

First edition for the United States, its territories and dependencies, and Canada published in 2013 by Barron's Educational Series, Inc.

© Copyright 2012 by Gemser Publications, S.L.
El Castell, 38, 08329 Teià, Barcelona, Spain

Text: Jennifer Moore-Mallinos
Illustration: Gustavo Mazali
Design and layout: Estudi Guasch, S.L.

All inquiries should be addressed to:
Barron's Educational Series, Inc.
250 Wireless Boulevard
Hauppauge, NY 11788
www.barronseduc.com

ISBN: 978-1-4380-0348-1

Library of Congress Control Number: 2013931782

Date of Manufacture: July 2013
Place of Manufacture: L. REX PRINTING COMPANY LIMITED,
Dongguan City, Guangdong, China

Product conforms to all applicable CPSC and CPSIA 2008 standards.
No lead or phthalate hazard.

Printed in China
9 8 7 6 5 4 3 2 1